Faster five runners,
Follow your dreams!
—Becca
777

To my daughter Taylor: I wrote this book for you. You're my biggest inspiration in life and when people ask me what I think about when I run, my answer is YOU. You are my number one cheerleader, and I'm SO lucky to be your mom.

To my parents Fred and Sue: "If my dreams don't scare my parents, they aren't big enough." Thank you for supporting my crazy dreams throughout the years.

To my twin sisters Lauren and Kristin: You're the best aunties in the world.

To my brother Mike: You're my favorite brother and best uncle to Tay.

To my nephews Matt and Justin: I'm so proud of you.

To my husband Joe: I hit the lottery with you, and thank you for believing in me.

www.mascotbooks.com

Becca's Feat on Feet

For more information, please contact:
Mascot Books
620 Herndon Parkway #320
Herndon, VA 20170
info@mascotbooks.com

Library of Congress Control Number: 2020900857

CPSIA Code: PRFRE0420A
ISBN-13: 978-1-64543-260-9

Printed in Canada

Becca's Feat on Feet

Becca Pizzi

illustrated by Marco Primo

Hi! I'm Becca, and I love to run. I run every single day, no matter what the New England weather brings. I ran my first race with my dad in my hometown of Belmont, Massachusetts when I was just six years old! Running is my passion and has taken me all around the world.

My favorite race distance is called a marathon, which is 26.2 miles long! That's as long as 461 football fields. The very first marathon I ran was the Boston Marathon. I grew up cheering for marathon runners from the famous Heartbreak Hill, and I'll never forget the first time I crossed the finish line on Boylston Street and received my medal.

Running this race is my annual tradition, and some of my favorite things about the Boston Marathon are the Boston Red Sox baseball game score updates along the route, the father/son running duo of Team Hoyt, the iconic Citgo sign, and the deafening crowd support throughout the eight towns along the way. It's always on Patriot's Day—Boston's favorite holiday!

3. North America
Miami - USA
42.195 Km

4. Europe
Madrid - Spain
42.195 Km

5. Afri
Marrakesh
42.195 Km

2. South America
Punta Arenas - Chile
42.195 Km

1. Antarctica
Union Glacier
42.195 Km

One day, I read about a race called the World Marathon Challenge. The race consists of running seven marathons on seven continents in seven days. That's 183.4 miles in just one week! From the freezing icecaps in Antarctica, to the hot desert lands of Africa, I would be pushed to my limits—and beyond. An American woman had never completed the race before.

Could I make history and be the first one?

When I asked my daughter Taylor if she thought I could do it, she jumped up and shouted, "YES! I believe in you, Mom. FINISH STRONG!" And that's how I got my motto from my *biggest* inspiration.

6. Asia
Dubai - UAE
42.195 Km

7. Australia
Sydney - Australia
42.195 Km

The first marathon was in Union Glacier, Antarctica. (Usually, only penguins live in Antarctica, but I actually got to visit.) To get there, we had to fly on a Russian Ilyushin, a military plane that could land us safely on a glacier. Glaciers are made of compact snow and ice, which is what we would be running on.

The wind was fierce and the sun was so bright, but the Antarctic ice-capped mountains were a nice distraction from the cold. I stayed focused and "finished strong!" I waved the American flag proudly when I crossed the finish line. One marathon down, six to go!

Hay Mommy
Maybe you can Try Some Chily in Chile if it's Chylly!

Love

Taylor

I left all the cold ice behind and moved on to my next continent: South America. I was so lucky to have friends and family on each continent to run with me and cheer me on. Their hugs and familiar faces were exactly what I needed, even more than aspirin or bandages. My friend Jenny ran the marathon with me in Punta Arenas, Chile. The course ran by the Strait of Magellan and having her by my side meant the world to me.

Taylor had written me a note to read after I crossed the finish line on each continent. This one read, **"If you're chilly in Chile, eat chili!"**—which was exactly what I did!

The third marathon took me to South Beach in Miami, Florida. I definitely had a home course advantage being back in the USA. More friends and family cheered for me along the course, including my college coach! We ran this marathon on the Miami boardwalk, with a lot of palm trees lining the course. After the marathon, I hugged my family and friends and was well on my way to accomplishing my goal.

I was about halfway through the challenge when I got to Europe for the fourth marathon. The rolling hills in Madrid, Spain, reminded me of Heartbreak Hill in Boston.

At Taylor's school, Wellington Elementary, she and her classmates were tracking my progress, and would even work on homework related to my journey. I got to video chat with Taylor's class from all over the world! (Except Antarctica—did you know they don't have Wi-Fi there? I called home on a satellite phone, instead!)

As soon as I finished the marathon in Madrid, it was on to the next continent. I was feeling confident but fatigue was setting in, so I remembered what my friend and mentor Warren Waugh, one of my marathon sponsors always says: **"WE GOT THIS."**

WELLINGTON
Elementary School

4. Europe
Madrid - Spain
42.195 Km

North Ameri...
...ami - USA
...95 Km

5. Africa
Marrakesh - Morocco
42.195 Km

6.
Dub...
42.19...

...h America
...ta Arenas - Chile
42.195 Km

1. Antarctica
Union Glacier
42.195 Km

Eat. Sleep. Fly. REPEAT.
We averaged ten hours flying per continent. Right when we'd land, I'd put on my running sneakers, change into my race gear, and go straight to the marathon. In between marathons, I'd focus on recovery and foam rolling.

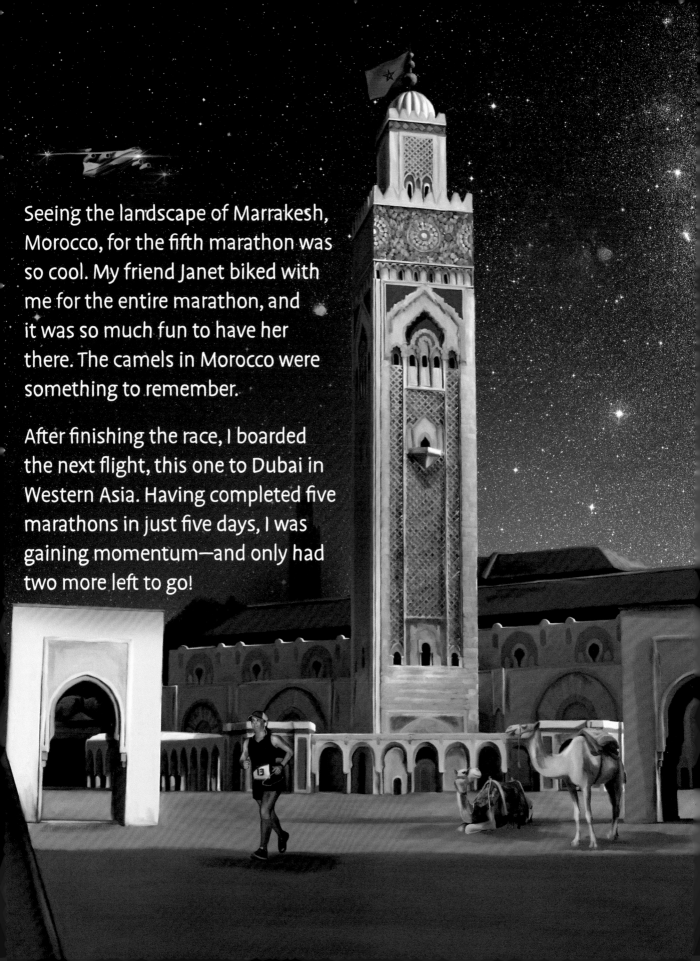

Seeing the landscape of Marrakesh, Morocco, for the fifth marathon was so cool. My friend Janet biked with me for the entire marathon, and it was so much fun to have her there. The camels in Morocco were something to remember.

After finishing the race, I boarded the next flight, this one to Dubai in Western Asia. Having completed five marathons in just five days, I was gaining momentum—and only had two more left to go!

Even though I was told many times that running seven marathons on seven continents in seven days was impossible, not finishing this race was not an option.

But my confidence was tested in Dubai, a city in the United Arab Emirates. I promised myself that even if I fell down at any point in the races, I would get back up and "finish strong." I injured myself and the pain was constant but I completed that marathon like I did every other: **one mile at a time.**

When I crossed the finish line, I felt as tall as the Burj Khalifa—the tallest building in the world, and one that I ran right past in Dubai!

When we landed in Australia for the final marathon, I was exhausted. **I was only 26.2 miles away** from accomplishing this feat. The crowd support from the Australians at midnight was awesome.

Crossing the finish line 10,086 miles away from home, with my family watching live on Skype, was something I will never forget. The first words out of my mouth when crossing the finish line were...

7 MARATHONS
7 CONTINENTS
7 DAYS

Lyon-Waugh
AUTO GROUP

...WE³

WORLD
MARATHON
CHALLENGE
7 MARATHONS
7 CONTINENTS
7 DAYS
22
WORLD
MARATHON
DID IT!

Making history by becoming the first American woman to cross the finish line on all seven continents was incredible! When I got back home to Belmont, the whole town came out to celebrate with me.

Congratulations, Becca Pizzi!
World Marathon Challenge Winner
Meet Becca on Thursday at 3:30 at Belmont Savings

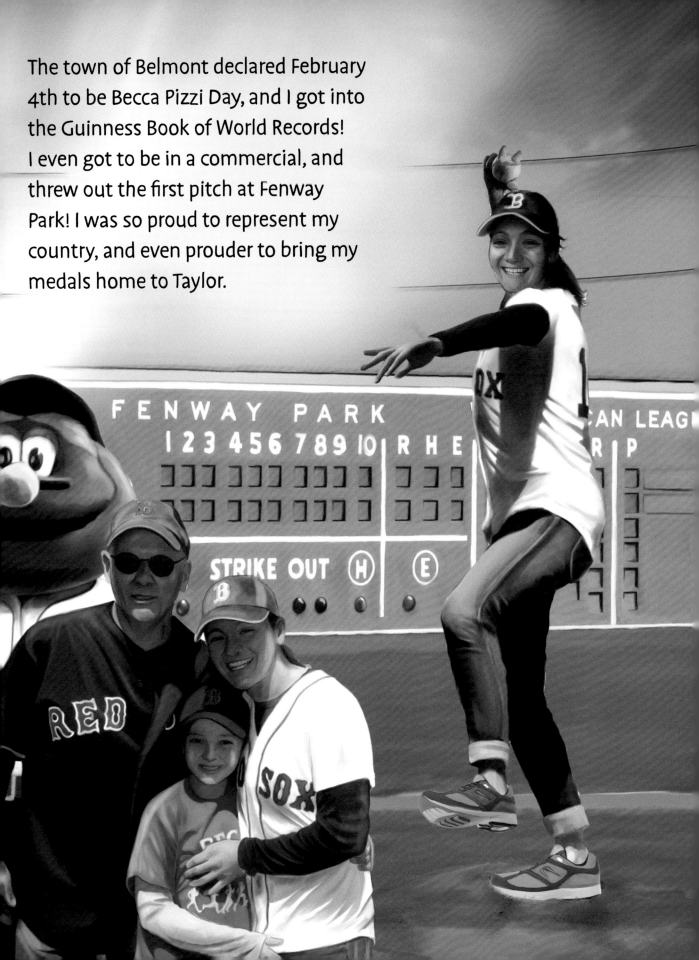

The town of Belmont declared February 4th to be Becca Pizzi Day, and I got into the Guinness Book of World Records! I even got to be in a commercial, and threw out the first pitch at Fenway Park! I was so proud to represent my country, and even prouder to bring my medals home to Taylor.

My advice to you is to find *your* World Marathon Challenge. Find whatever it is that you are passionate about. **Dream big, take chances,** and always believe in yourself. Because, when you do, *anything* is possible.

GUINNESS WORLD RECORDS

CERTIFICAT

The fastest time to comp
marathon on each of the
continents by a female is 6
hr 38 min and was achiev
Becca Pizzi (USA) in Sydn
South Wales, Australia, fro
30 January 2016.

OFFICIALLY AMAZIN

RECORD HO

HOME
GUEST
DOWN
TO GO
BALL ON
QTR.
HOME OF
THE BELMONT MARAUDERS
BELMONT HIGH
MARAUDERS

BECCA PIZZI ANNUAL 5K

About the Author

Becca grew up in Belmont, Massachusetts, where she lives with her husband, Joe, and her daughter, Taylor. She graduated from Belmont High School in 1998. She loves the Belmont community and credits her success to Belmont for inspiring her to do her best. She is a Six Star Finisher of the World Marathon Majors, a series of six of the largest and most renowned marathons in the world. The Boston Marathon is her favorite marathon, and she has run it sixteen times! Becca is on track to complete a marathon in all fifty states. She is most passionate about directing the Becca Pizzi 5k race in Belmont, and loves seeing her community come together to support Belmont High School athletes.

www.beccapizzi.com